AF375209

Gigi Matka

Takes A Stand

Gigi Matka

Takes A Stand

*A call to become
more of who you
really are*

Story by Betsy Sheppard

Illustrations by Layne Sovereign

Gigi Matka Takes a Stand

Published by Wisdom House Books, Inc.
Wilmington, North Carolina 28401 USA
www.wisdomhousebooks.com

Wisdom House Books is committed to excellence
in the publishing industry.

Book design copyright © 2026 Wisdom House Books, Inc.
Cover and interior design by Ted Ruybal
Illustrations by Layne Sovereign

Printed in the United States of America
Hardback ISBN: 979-8-9953781-0-5
LCCN: 2026909151

FIC010000 | FICTION / Fairy Tales, Folk Tales, Legends & Mythology
FIC009010 | FICTION / Fantasy / Contemporary
FIC009080 | FICTION / Fantasy / Humorous

First Edition

25 24 23 22 21 20 / 10 9 8 7 6 5 4 3 2 1

Dedication

For my children, your children,
and all children everywhere.

Author's Note

Why Gigi? Why Now? Because this moment in time requires more from all of us. We must remember what we have forgotten about being human together.

Humans have amazing behavioral flexibility. And sometimes, we get stuck in a pattern of beliefs and behaviors that is self-destructive, individually and collectively. Today, we are over-emphasizing some innate qualities at the expense of other essential aspects of being human—power over wisdom, self-righteousness over unconditional love, busyness over stillness, arrogance over wonder.

It doesn't have to be this way. The qualities we need to meet the challenges we face may be suppressed, sidelined, and overshadowed, but they are not lost. We retain access to a shared, universal memory of what it means to be human. If we shift our attention and awareness, we can activate, balance and integrate all essential aspects of the human experience.

The purpose of this book is to start a conversation about what we really value and about who we choose to be. The intent with the Gigi character is to provide a playful, inviting entry point for examining fundamental questions about human nature and for redefining what is normal, what is moral, and what is possible in how we live together.

Sadly, we have become more fearful, brittle versions of who we really are—unable to fully embrace life. In times of great uncertainty, complexity, and rapid change, it is easy to blame others and point the finger at the enemy out there. It is easy to turn against one another and to retreat to the safety of our own tribe. It is hard to look inside yourself and confront the hidden assumptions and beliefs you hold about who and how you are supposed to be. It is hard to accept the role we all play in creating the reality we experience. The patterns of beliefs and behaviors that hold us back individually are the same patterns that hold us back collectively.

We all want a better, more peaceful world for our children and their children. When we reclaim our own innate power and potential, we help restore hope for the future. "I matter" and "we belong together" are inextricably linked.

Who might we be if we began walking toward a truer understanding of ourselves and our relationship with the world around us? Gigi Matka is here to guide us and help us pause, take a stand and become more of who we really are.

The View From Above

Oh my. Things are not going well on planet Earth. People are anxious, lonely, fearful, angry, and cynical. They are harming themselves, harming others, and harming the beautiful blue planet they call home.

I'm Gigi Matka, the Mother of all life. I'm a source of creative life-giving energy, unconditional love, and connection to the Earth, to all living beings and to the wisdom of the universe. Unfortunately, in this modern age of machines, algorithms and artificial intelligence, people are losing access to sacred human gifts of awe, wonder, beauty, intuition, compassion, humility and reverence for the mystery and miracle of life.

If I could wave a magic wand, I'd take everyone back in time to when they were very young and in love with the world. They would remember what it felt like to squeal with delight and jump for joy, to have fiery determination and wild imagination. They could recapture that feeling of being radically alive.

I get it. People are busy with their lives. It's not easy to make your way in the world, to take care of yourself and your loved ones. As social beings, you conform to fit in and be accepted by others, you seek approval and validation, and you long to be needed and loved.

Sadly, the cost of this social pressure is that humans learn to hide and repress essential aspects of their true nature. Over time they become a more faded, a more jaded, a more superficial version of themselves. I just want to shout at the top of my lungs, "you are so much more than who you are allowing yourselves to be!"

But yelling probably won't do any good if no one is paying attention. Perhaps there is another way that I could help people see who they really are—help them rediscover what it's like to be in the world in the fullness of their humanity.

I know . . . how about a hotline? People could reach out to me when they feel stuck, alone, lost, and in need of someone to talk to. Honest conversation and self-exploration are a great way to uncover what gets in the way of expressing your innate potential. I'll make it really easy for everyone—a toll-free, 24/7, cosmic hotline (fastest connection in the Universe), available anywhere you happen to be.

Maybe this is a crazy idea. But I guess it's worth a shot. You never know until you try.

Conditional
Love

Jingle Jingle. Wow, that was quick. Gigi Matka here. How can I be of service?

Hi there. I'm Lana from Little Rock. I haven't been able to sleep all night, tossing and turning. And then, I saw this sparkling silver bell with a note on it. So, I rang it and I guess it connected me with you. I sure would love someone to talk to.

Hi Lana. I'm so happy you called. I've kind of lived forever and have learned many valuable lessons to share. What's troubling you?

I find myself constantly trying to please others at the expense of my own needs and interests. And, then I beat myself up, "why can't you just stand up for yourself Lana and say no sometimes." I feel like such a doormat, getting trampled on all the time. Why am I so weak?

My dear Lana, you have more strength and determination than you realize. It's just "offline" at the moment. All humans struggle at times with an underlying fear of rejection and abandonment. This fear can be like a relentless inner critic that makes you feel flawed and unlovable. It can trick you into believing that you'll only be loved if you make others happy.

Wow, that type of fear seems hard to get rid of. What can I do?

Let's start by giving that nagging voice a name. How about Doormat Daisy? Naming these deep fears and bringing them into the light is a good way to confront them so they no longer have power over you. Pretending they are not there never works.

Oh, I see. How's this for a picture of Doormat Daisy?

Wonderful. The next step is to practice loving yourself. Your perceived imperfections are features not flaws. They are what make you the unique person that you are.

Self-doubt and insecurity are normal aspects of the human condition. The hurt you feel is the same hurt hidden inside others as well. Loving and accepting your pain helps you live with it, not try to get rid of it. How about a daily affirmation, "even though I sometimes feel unworthy of love, I deeply and profoundly love and accept myself as I am."

You know what, I feel a little better already. Doormat Daisy may still make an appearance from time to time, but now I'll acknowledge her and let her go on her way. I will not let her define me.

That's the way to get started Lana.

Keep at it!

How about a cosmic hug.

Till next time.

I'm always here for you.

Power Play

Look at me, a titan of industry and here l am alone trying to find something to watch among the thousands of streaming options available. Here's something l've never seen before: GigiNow. Hmm, it seems to be free, no sign-in required.

Thanks for connecting to the Cosmic Hotline. l'm Gigi and whom do l have the pleasure of speaking with?

l'm Zed from Olympia, Gigi. l was at a loss of what to do with myself this evening when l stumbled upon this channel.

It seems like you could use a friend to talk to Zed, As the Mother of all life, I've seen and heard it all. What's bothering you?

I was married for a long time and I have a teenage daughter, Kora. My wife Denise and I had a major falling out that caused us to go our separate ways. Now, I live by myself and just work, work, work to hide the hurt I feel from losing Denise and Kora, the people I love most in the world.

Yes, divorce can be painful for all involved. Relationships with loved ones are always worth saving though, no matter what has happened in the past. Can you share with me what led to the blow up?

I've led a very successful life as founder and CEO of multiple companies. There was a time when I thought that I could do nothing wrong. I felt powerful, respected and always on top of my game. Yet at the same time, I had difficulty dealing with anyone who tried to question my knowledge and authority.

It can be hard being the big boss, Zed. There is a lot of pressure to appear confident and in control at all times, never wanting to look weak or indecisive. How did this work pressure impact your homelife?

Besides working constantly, I also had trouble turning off my power persona with Denise and Kora. I could be quite the hothead, prone to angry outbursts over little things. I was absent a lot, physically and emotionally, and I became jealous of their close relationship. Instead of listening and learning about what was going on in their lives, I was forceful and tried to impose my views of right and wrong.

I bet you were hard to tolerate when laying down the law without any regard for the perspective, needs and aspirations of Denise and Kora.

Yes, I hate to admit it, but I continued to push them away. Until one day, I went too far. I decided that Denise, and especially Kora, were becoming too bold for their own good. So, I made a deal with the headmaster at Perfect Angel Boarding School to accept Kora. I lied and told her that we were going on a fun trip together and dropped her off. I didn't feel the need to talk to my wife about it since I knew what was best. When Denise found out about this, I knew we were done. Twenty-five years of marriage down the drain due to my own insecurity.

It sounds like you have reflected on this quite a bit, Zed, and learned some valuable lessons.

Well, what really helped me is the kindness and forgiveness that Denise offered me. She continued to love me despite my past behavior. Her compassion and grace taught me the true meaning of courage and gave me the strength to admit my mistakes.

It is nice to see that you are calmer and more at ease. Continue to practice noticing when your need to control flares up. Then connect to the love you feel for others and that same love will be returned to you.

Lost in
the Woods
22

How on earth did I get here? I have no idea where I am or what to do. It's getting dark and cold—I feel some panic creeping in. Wait a minute . . . what is this silver bell doing here in the woods? Ring, ring, anyone there?

Gigi at your service.

Am I in a dream? What am I doing in the middle of the woods? And, who are you?

Well, I am the Mother of all life, Gigi Matka. My hotline started buzzing as your heart rate accelerated. What's your name and how can I help?

Hi Gigi. I'm Quinn from Quincy. I just don't know what's going on with me or how exactly I got myself lost in the woods. Each day I wake up with this weird sense of living someone else's life. I struggle sometimes to get through the day as though I'm sleepwalking through my life.

Hmm, sounds familiar. Is this a new feeling or has it been around for a while?

Well, to tell you the truth I've always tried to be who others thought I should be. When my own ideas and aspirations creep in, I just dismiss them as foolish fantasies. No one can afford to daydream these days or you'll end up a nobody—left out and left behind.

No wonder you feel disoriented, Quinn. It can be really hard when society dictates who and how you should be. You find yourself trying to live up to some external standard that feels impossible to meet.

Yeah, like the goal posts keep moving further away the closer you get. And I don't even know why I'm trying to get there. What is the point??

The missing piece for many people, especially in the middle of life, is a connection to their deeper self: their soul identity. All human beings have their own particular genius —a unique imprint to make on the world. Unfortunately, the pressure of societal expectations causes people to repress and hide their most precious gifts.

That makes sense Gigi, but it can be difficult to find your way in the world. It seems naïve to just follow your own desires.

Yes, it can be difficult to find the right balance between surviving and thriving. Yet the simple truth is, learning to walk where your inner self wants to go doesn't have to be about some grandiose achievement. Rather, it's about how much of your essence you can reveal and bring forth in small ways, in everyday moments, and in how you live your life.

I don't really know who I am because I've never stopped to think about it. I guess that is why I feel lost.

No worries, Quinn. Wherever you are in your life, you can learn to follow your own path, to sing your own tune. You can start by taking time each day to be still, be quiet, pay attention and listen deeply to your inner wisdom. You may notice recurring themes or patterns to your insights and yearnings. Journaling can be helpful to reflect upon what you are deeply, intuitively drawn toward. Everyone has access to their own inner GPS, like breadcrumbs leading you out of the dark forest.

Thanks Gigi. It may take some time to find my way, but I think I'm pointed in the right direction. I'll make sure to pause along the way to pay attention to my inner GPS.

Anywhere but here

Another ordinary day, ponders Jerri . . . where can I escape to for some excitement?

Wow what is this GigiNow option? I didn't even know these glasses had this setting.

Hi Jerri. Welcome to the Cosmic Couch. Drop in guests are always welcome.

Ah..hi there. I don't know what's happening here, but I'm game. Where am I and who are you?

I am the Mother of all life and I'm pleased to be in conversation with you here in my cosmic perch. You can call me Gigi.

Cool. Nice to meet you, Gigi. I was having another day of the same old, same old . . . some work, some video clips, some scrolling, some commenting. You know . . . modern life. Sometimes I feel so bored and disinterested in my life. It can all seem so phony and meaningless, trying to keep up with things that I don't even care about.

I hear you, Jerri. You are not alone in this sentiment. People today are bombarded with information and pulled in many different directions. Your attention is scattered all over the place, never fully doing one thing at a time. Sometimes you need a place to land and truly be where you are.

Yeah, everyone is clamoring to break through the noise to get noticed, to stand out, and to feel relevant. It's exhausting having to perform all the time. Sometimes I just can't take it, so I connect to some other reality.

In this screen-filled digital age, it can be hard to find ways to experience wonder, beauty, and awe. Digital experiences alone will not suffice. Let me ask you Jerri, when was the last time you felt excited to be alive, delighted by simple things, and absorbed in the present moment?

I don't know, maybe when I was a kid. Sure sounds nice.

Don't give up on your "aliveness." I promise you it's far more fascinating than anything virtual could ever be. The world is full of astonishment, in every moment and in every direction. I believe that you're up to the task of living Jerri, you're just a little out of practice. Start by taking time each day to be enthralled by the miracle of life all around you, to notice the extraordinary in the ordinary. Then maybe, you won't feel the need to escape anymore.

Thanks Gigi. I think I can fit those moments into my busy schedule. Just kidding. Can you teleport me home please? I'll let you borrow the glasses.

Leap of Faith

Wow, these conversations have really boosted my spirits. I get so excited when I envision people expressing self-compassion and compassion for all teamed up with fierce determination and courageous action. I feel over the moon about the possibility of everyone tapping into their inner wisdom while opening themselves up to the mystery and miracle of life itself. Oh what a world it would be if people let go of their self-imposed limitations and felt free to express all their innate and essential human capacities!

Here I go again, getting carried away with myself. Time to slow down, Gigi. Yes, I wish you all could sit here next to me and see what I see. But that is not how it works. No mother can direct and mold her children into who she thinks they should be and could be. I know that everyone must embark on their own journey of self-discovery. All

I can do is offer inspiration and encouragement for the road ahead.

The simple truth is that these conversations are just the beginning, a small glimpse into what you may be missing. The lost aspects of yourself are not gone forever, they are just buried under years of social conditioning. These hidden capacities can be activated when needed and to be blunt, NOW would definitely be a good time.

The hard part is having the courage to be brutally honest with yourself. Start by hitting the pause button in the movie of your life. Notice that the voice in your head directing the show is NOT who you really are. Put a stake in the ground and ask some tough questions.

What do you really want? What is worth living for? How do you want to treat others and be treated? If you could be more of who you are, all of who you are, what are you capable of?

"Whoa, Gigi, that's a lot to take in," you may be thinking. True, but there is no exam here, no time limit to come up with the answers. The power is in the asking. Your task is to just follow the questions wherever they take you with great determination and great faith. The faith to face your fears and go forward anyway into the unknown with no clear path to follow.

The next chapter in the story of your life is not yet written. And no one can write it for you. As you set out on your journey, I offer one key nugget of motherly advice: "don't fly solo." Remember to turn toward one another, not away or against. You all share the same human struggles and yearnings: to love and be loved, to determine your own path, to express your natural creative energy, and to celebrate the miracle of being alive.

Let's keep the conversation going and see where it takes us . . .

Reflection and Discussion:
Remembering What We Have Forgotten About Being Human Together

Task 1 Individual Noticing: Who Do I Choose to Be?

We all have hidden fears and self-imposed limitations that hold us back from becoming more of who we are meant to be. These common pitfalls of conditional self-acceptance can be thought of as, "I'll be ok if . . ." Begin to notice and reflect upon the ways in which you might undermine your full and honest expression across these four essential qualities of the human experience.

Unconditional Love: compassion for self, others, all living beings, and the whole of nature. Potential limiting beliefs: I'll only be loved if . . . I don't anger and upset others. I am perfect and pulled together. I go along to get along. I am wanted and needed by taking care of others and not myself.

How does it feel to maintain this acquiescent stance and who might you become without it?

Personal Power: autonomy, agency, and fierce determination.
Potential limiting beliefs: I'll only be admired if . . . I am not dependent on others. I appear strong and in control. I am forceful and hide any perceived weakness.

How does it feel to maintain this dominant stance and who might you become without it?

Inner Guidance: imagination, intuition, creativity.
Potential limiting beliefs: I'll only belong if . . . I meet others' expectations. I don't take unnecessary risks. I conform to societal beliefs and norms.

How does it feel to maintain this compliant stance and who might you become without it?

Being Here Now: wonder, joy, beauty.
Potential limiting beliefs: I'll only be happy if . . . If I tune out the noise around me. If I stay busy and don't waste my time on silly things. If I avoid surprises and spontaneity.

How does it feel to maintain this restrictive stance and who might you become without it?

Important Note: Humor and self-compassion are essential. Noticing our human ways, frailties, and fixations is nourishing but unsettling. A little laughter and kind-heartedness goes a long way.

Task 2 Collective Noticing: How Do We Want to Live Together?

The patterns of beliefs and behaviors that hold us back individually also hold us back as a society. These self-destructive patterns prevent us from facing current reality and making shared sacrifices for the greater good. Yes, we all matter as unique individuals, yet we are also part of and contribute to a larger interdependent whole. Keep in mind, "hurting others hurts myself."

In your book club, your friend groups, your community gatherings, your places of worship take time to slow down and engage in conversation about what matters most. Turn toward one another to explore what a healthier, more wholehearted society might look like. Here are some sample questions. Pick one or two that resonate with the group.

- What does success look like?
- What is real wealth?
- What is a life well-lived?
- What does moral courage look like?
- What truly delights you? What frightens you?
- What do we need more of? What do we need less of?

Acknowledgements

Special thanks to Carol S. Pearson, author of Persephone Rising and What Stories Are You Living?, and Margaret J. Wheatley, author of Leadership and the New Science and Who Do We Choose to Be?, for their kindness, wisdom, and encouragement on my own journey of becoming more of who I really am.

About the Author

Betsy Shepprd is a co-producing author of Adventures in Reinventing Work—Tales of Pioneers from Around the World. She lives in North Carolina with her husband of 35 years and their notorious chihuahua mix Diesel.

About the Illustrator

Layne Sovereign graduated from the University of North Carolina at Greensboro with a Bachelor's degree in Fine Arts and a concentration in animation. She lived in Japan and Germany as a child, which greatly influenced her artistic style and interests, such as fairytales. She loves to experiment with whimsical, romantic, medieval, and gothic elements in her own personal art.